All the Fires
of Wind and Light

All the Fires
of Wind and Light

MAYA KHOSLA

SIXTEEN RIVERS PRESS

Published by Sixteen Rivers Press
P.O. Box 640663
San Francisco, CA 94164-0663
www.sixteenrivers.org

Library of Congress Control Number: 2018953098
ISBN: 978-1939639-19-6

Cover and interior photos: Maya Khosla
Author photo: Joyce Ambrosius
Book design: Beth Spencer

For the Fire Strategy Group, whose members understand climate change, the value of natural wildfire, and why we need to preserve the ecosystems we have.

CONTENTS

THE CONVERSION OF SUN INTO MEMORY

OF THE FORESTS AFTER FIRE

THE CONVERSION OF SUN
INTO MEMORY

DISPERSAL

Cicadas dedicate their piercing calls to the stars:
      tireless desire pitched into the jeweled universe
            with the most power a chorus of cells can muster.

Such surges are rooted in the core of oaks, native
      to the multi-million nuclei within each being.
            To the fledgling dread of a falcon, preparing

for first flight. To an apple's thump on earth,
      kernels of yearning sealed in the double darkness
            of sugars and night-rose skin speckled with sun.

All store formulae for longing and reaching with genetic perfection,
      for surviving the conflagrations of the ages and gleaming
            with newness. All preserve themselves at a cost.

After the water is filtered, tent pegs fastened,
      the apple sliced, the forest stilled,
            I enter that world one mouthful at a time.

Along the mountain's rim, the lapping grasses
      are lighter for the absence of prickly seed-heads
            quick-released into my socks as I passed.

SYNCHRONICITY

In Bhutan, my camera's *click* jerks a mother yak
from her suckling young. I forget to lower myself

into stillness, how it calms animals. Miles up-mountain
a goatherd struggling to lift her dead goat, stuck

in blue junipers, finds a snow leopard jawing the head.
As I reach for a cupful of darkness, a half-human

half-animal yowl creates a blue bowl of sound.
Blood is a clock looking back as it advances. Ancestors

mourn for a departed son in sixteenth century silence
while a kite swoops down on his lit funeral pyre.

A man walks up switchbacks of asphalt not knowing
the bison have broken loose from the fenced savannah ahead.

Dawn's butterflies alight on pines miles from home
while the yak herders say the yowl was *not sasquatch,*

maybe leopard. Tasting the words, we feel like prey,
seesawing between fear and surrender.

The air is brisk. Hunger switches
from perch to perch on chilled wings.

Deep in a village brawl, a child is torn off its mother's back
like a postage stamp. Coffee steam, from a cup I grip

on a rooftop, joins smoke from the sunlit bazaar.
Thunder rolls along the tree-line. Mountains don't answer

the goatherd singing for the rest of her flock. Guard dogs
barking after the leopard's departure swell its silence.

IN KABUL

Candlelight skids up the child who sleepwalks with eyes wide.
Airwaves lower than sound or shudder rattle cups
and doors. In her dream, trees cling to their blood apricots

swollen with the darkness of curfew nights.
Touch one and it explodes. Her father's vigil is crumpled
by insomnia: was that wind-shift or voices shrilling

above the crack of footfalls beyond view? It is the hour of curtains
jerked from grip. Out there, gloved hands are setting down
landmines the shape of toys. By morning, miles of window glass

lie glittering, chips of sun. A layer of dust on every cup of water.
After the one p.m. car bomb, the front door falls toward her father
as he pulls it open. It is another month. The child's coat slumped

against a tree. He is searching for her. He wants to tell her
about the bent limbs, the elbows of trunk, the way it leans
against granitic rocks, gestures fortified by nutrients and hope.

Parted clouds brighten a shrike balanced on a stalk. Swaying
back and forth, its body keeps a tempo of hunger against
the valley's great backdrop strewn with silences.

The slow ache of sky sinking through his search.
Now a chewed-up fruit with her tooth marks. Arrows of distress
scatter like night-birds from the open mouth of falling.
Now wind whistling, a half-shout running through it.

BLUE OAK

A meadow ends where all the perpendiculars
river throw themselves up towards blue.
and ocher. Sprays of dark leaves
sun. Lightning scars show where
by flames, was not lost but reduced
under sheets of earth, sleeping
of quick-heat. Here it is: the world
the anguish, despite endless battles.
slipped away to yours. My phone is still
back. I could babble about this testimony
limbs and great elbows of trunk leaning
gestures of pondering and reconciliation.
the looping and fluttering of flycatchers,
fog-drip and shade, pressed flat where a fox
doglike circles round and round   before
hold up my phone among the workings of xylem
so you could hear the rustling, the liquid flow
out of the heart's rocky sloping, terrain
only a river can. Or I could stand still

of a leafy brown
The fruits are olive
shiver and splash with
the main, once shaped
to fine fists, oak tissue
through the storm and teeth
utterly lovely despite
Meanwhile, you have
again. I could call
to resilience, bent
against granite in
I could share
grasses fresh with
recently turned
settling in. I could
and phloem
scooping minutes
and flowing on as
and listen.

AMAZING GRACE

The leader sings it, and all rise. Singing of the hush. Singing of tumult, of daylight sucked from stained-glass windows. The song like a storm roaring between past and present, entering each singer as an anthem of faith, emerging as dirge. Each singer an island, an orphaned silence, filled. The nine named over and over so all remain with us. The whispers. The moment the walls turned into paper and shook with light. The books lying open, the dark drops. Dust bits hanging in a slant of sun. Late light flooding the floor with color. The light making contact, splitting one irrevocable moment from the next. Now the song as memory, as the means of counting the vanished one by one without numbers. Arriving at nine and unable to go beyond. What is lost, replenished by grace. Each mouth full of words incinerated, yet carrying on. For none of the extinguished will go voiceless. Mouths full of vespers will sing of them. A thousand songs. Faces and candles from here to the horizon, and onward. The hymn multiplying into a living continent of song. All will continue to sing it. All will rise.

President Obama sang in memory of the nine people
who lost their lives in the 2015 Charleston massacre.

WON'T FUSS, WON'T CRY

There is cheese, a red bowl of olives. A circle of hands
working the loaves and cumin-dotted butterfish
clouded with spices and salt, the rivers of distance
they have come to represent. Slivers of steam rise like auguries,
pressing against windows yellow-gold with evening lamps.
Outside, a sky of pimiento and flame lingers. An old twinge

invites the heart out. It is neither the ache of remembering
history's boots crushing fresh-tilled hopes, nor the years
of shrinking beneath the weight of fear. Neither the set of dishes
piled high as afterthoughts to cover the one with a crack
too deep for repair, nor the radio voice warbling *Won't fuss,*

won't cry. No. This is the heart needing to depart
from company for a moment, fending off the past,
emerging to brush against bunchgrass and fir veiled
in lunar light. To listen for the thud of acorns dropping
from oaks grown ripe with the conversion of sun

into memory. This is the heart tasseled in cirrocumulus,
touching the cicatrix, the bark tender with loss.
It glides past regret toward the river in search
of itself—amid the debris of driftwood and stone,
the journey that has given good distance.

At the Wellspring Retreat

QUILTING, A REFUGEE REMEMBERS HER HOME
BEFORE THE DAM WAS BUILT

Cross-legged on the floor of the makeshift factory,
bent over blues and vermilions, she takes one scrap
of herself and another. Stitches them edge to edge:
all the sunny luxuries, all the promises cracked

and banished to high ground, bundles of belongings
on heads and shoulders, backs turned on the gray chains
of concrete tying waters to expanding waters, the village
slipping under. Bent low, she picks up one snapshot,

another. Bright seeds of amaranth held in women's scarves,
salvaged window frames in the arms of men. A brass god
carried by two. Bent low, her eyes are transfixed by faces
dissolving beneath the surface tension

binding cloth to cloth, folds soaking with darkness, ruin,
and the muddy turbidities of exile. Bent over the valleys
and hideouts, she is stitching the trickle through fields
of red rice, a tangle of flowers bowing and nodding

under the weight of butterflies alive for a whorl of days
before pressing themselves close to soaked earth.
Here are the threads of heartland to be bartered away.
Here an altar knocked loose. And here is a woman

wading into her home, waist deep in darkness.
Keys tied to the end of her sari. The rising waters
crank and moan. The pieces that must be gathered up
are slipping from her mind.

> *"We will drown but we will not move"; we have no choice
> but to keep repeating this.* —Medha Patkar

PILGRIMAGE TO COW'S MOUTH MOUNTAIN

In a time of ice, a time before glaciers began retreating
and Mount Everest began losing whole feet
of height to the world's rising heat, four men walked
carrying a curtained palanquin. Hidden inside,
my grandmother sat with her clutch of sketching pencils,

a sheaf of paper. First light brushed a cold burn
against blue snows miles above touch. They climbed
toward headwaters, boulders the size of cabins.
Closed in where the Ganges River roared
down rapids. Skin of fire and body of darkness

carving canyons into stone flour, silty riches,
and banks full of chestnut trees and edelweiss.
My grandmother steps into the spray. Enters
the blue hallways, the generations of song.
The skirts of her sari balloon out, then cling.

Toes sink into sand. The blue-gold everywhere.
Her teeth are chattering. Thirst and cold become one.
Eyes, head, and hands in prayer. *Give me the strength to live
without walls.* Mica bits glitter as they fly downstream.

GOLDEN EAGLE

Flight is a gaunt hunger let loose, working the lands
from ridge to ridge. Neck craned, her gaze is taut

as the sky's lion light. The stretched-open wings
full as sails shifting angles. Twelve feet from tip

to tip, she is almost unflappable, curled along the edges
where thermals spiral up. The whole body bronzed

in sun, the rippling meadows of brightness below
afloat on the notion of extended wings.

July's slopes have gone crisp, rippling with tinsel-sounds,
miner's lettuce, the dry music of wallflowers,

the bleached and the frayed, the grasses snapping
into themselves. Wind reveals well-squirreled trails

like pencil lines, erased and re-sketched over and over.
Now she swoops. This is when flight is the fastest heat,

intention combining the body's light and the mind
darkening all but the drop.

Let X be the point of the slam. Talons lock
on a flurry of fur, the squirming, the giving in.

Let Y be wedged deep in mid-level branches,
a luminous eyrie, her clutch of newborns cloaked in down.

AFTER DONATING ONE OF HER KIDNEYS

to save a life, she wakes to see crowns of cottonwoods
reaching for clouds aflame with light. Icy winds slipping
between leaves, low angles of gold slicing through.
A cold sun, birds gathering to chip at the flinty cones.
Watching their flickering, she feels the inner magnet

that will soon propel them to snap ties with the known,
venture across the unknown. The north-south orientation
of hope drawing their cries, their long lines across the sky.
Many are young, flying the mind's blind inclinations
for the first time, tasting the tough salts of Jetstream and fear.

To rise after parting with the body's inner sense
of bilateral symmetry is to understand that nothing
is annihilated; a little goes elsewhere. Migration
is the mind in storm, the mind prepared
to shed all but the vector between given and received,

between an emptied landscape and one rich
with nutrients, thimbleberries baked close to the quick
by solar heat. Still, there's no denying the half-emptiness
remaining. She lingers at the edge of what sang
along the slant of branches now swept clean.

For R. Schwartz

COMING TO TERMS WITH THE TERMINAL

The table between us is rickety, the ceiling coal black.
You've zipped up my flame-red dress. Dogs that yapped hard
into the sinking light are now calmer than candles in glass.

It is the time of comets, a dreamless time. Flames spit gold,
their choruses roaring. Drying, your shirt fills the room
with scents of fish scales and caddisfly cocoons
fashioned from quartz bits and waterproof glue.

We have turned our backs on the hospital rooms, the drips

that filled your veins with cisplatin and sickness, the hope
burning like a dim lamp at the end of a long hallway.
The world feels fluid. Whatever the river cracked open

continues to surge. Trout are slit quickly from the heart downward,

then salted. Winter is not empty-handed, just stiffer. Red saps
have turned from sticky toffee to rock. Cerulean warblers are gone.
Boiled light is sipped, a cross-country train is remembered.

We use cooking oil for our thorn-scratched arms. Outside,

a hemisphere of migrating wings turns the season south. Birds
whirring up, riding a river of insects. Our leafless willows crave
their shapes. But we have come to terms with the swell of darkness.

Parting fish flesh from bone, you watch it fall like a net full of rain.

For Gouri Khosla

12

SUBSIDENCE

The pulse still mid-sprint, the phone cradle still
tepid, a few minutes past loss. Then subsidence,
while the ocean's crimsoning distances tap

at the windows. Hesitant, perhaps needing entry.
You will not answer to the knocking this time.
A great weight has been lifted out
like a tide full of seaweed. Exposed, it is pungent
with salts and hubris. Never mind. Time now
to peel the just-bloomed mushrooms,
dice the overripe tomatoes,
skillet them with ginger slivers, coriander, honey,

the pop and fizzle of mustard seeds and salt.
Outside, the light tires, windows blur
with the heat of relish. Allow the nourishment
to be temple, juice, essential electrolyte.
Swallow its canto.

THUMBPRINT

The moment was all window. He drove off the mountain's edge
while bending to gather peanuts from the passenger seat.
Soothsayers who read my sister's thumbprint days before,

holding a bamboo leaf over the inky oval, had predicted the fall.
They spoke of glass blocking sky and floor. The call from hospital
roars with static. She listens through the long-distance crackle,

fears plunging towards the single fir that halted her love's drop.
A spinney of firs, verticals swaying, married to sun and river.
Further down, gravelly rapids dashing to white shards one moment,

seamless the next. The call done, silences grow from small sounds.
Branches, a fly beating against glass. Leaf stuck in a cobweb,
tapping out reports from far winds. Sweeping them all up,

she burns the predictions. But random words continue
to surge from the rising ash. *Amethyst, dove, bone.*
The mountain hospital is without anesthetics, needles disinfected

over flame. He returns to a monsoon without rain. A squash
from the farmers' market, carried home in his good hand,
swells so large it forces the refrigerator door open and rolls out.

She hears the soothsayers' chants hovering over the inky-dark oval
of her impression on paper. Holds her knowledge like a tablespoon
of Epsom salts, fizzing on her tongue without a drink to wash it down.

BAKING

Instructions live long past a life: the known creek
more honeyed than the new. I follow the flow
of my mother's scrawl, suggestion without insistence,
past great bottles in rows. Medicinal lemons
with their summaries of sun, sodium chloride crystals,
and quartered fruits, skin and seeds pickled to softness.

Mynahs cackle outside the kitchen window, competing
with neighbors shouting about the shortage of water.
"Fighting?" My sister shakes her head, laughs
as she squeezes past to turn off the water purifier.
The counters are packed. Oils, spices, half-inch ants
must be moved to make room for kneading.
Space is scarce, but I can take shelter elsewhere,

in another time. The ritual seemed to issue
from my mother's fingertips. Sundays, we kids eager
as she spooned soft butter, folded the salt, flour, air.
Then the caraway seeds. Heat printed crimsons
into the rising while we watched through the oven's
oil-bright window. Scents swelled. She tapped hot loaves
for hollow sounds. *Done.*

I have her knuckles. My dough is growing again.
What is pulled and punched down rises again
with resilience and cobalt-blue heat. The shape
of regeneration arranged by flames is well rounded.
With every loss, we gather closer.
We make sound and heat hum together.
The oven door is opened; hands and face
are warmed by all that rises to meet us.

REUSE, RENEWAL

We were raised in days of reuse, yogurt thickened with starch
from shredded newspapers. The Buddha's eyes painted half-closed,

the silver of listening bright on his eyelids. We were raised
to consume the wormless halves of apples, dip rusk into tea,

hire the *dhunai wala* who ripped open old quilts for reworking.
He traveled from house to house. Left his bicycle outside and squatted

to whisk the cotton guts out, wrap them around the cord
of a one-stringed instrument whose pluck would fluff up the wads.

One by one, helixes of cotton spreading into a blur of light
like whipped egg-whites or clouds in a sudden blaze of sun.

The single-note overture twanged on and on, giving shape to entropy,
the opposite of weave. The work of seasons, storage, suppressed hopes,

all undone. If a cotton-seed escaped its parent mist, it went ignored.
What mattered was that air, the gauzy keeper of heat,

would be stitched back into the silky darkness. What mattered
was the river's ice-tongues, collected in buckets of water,

would keep milk cold and good. Mornings we stayed chin deep
in the fluffed quilts, waiting for sun. Spread yak's butter on toast.

Carved from a conch shell on cliffs facing our window,
the Buddha's face attained silences deeper than snowfields.

NEW YEAR BETWEEN COUNTRIES

Lighting the bonfire without kindling takes hours,
hot rum, honey, and fizzy water. Flames are coaxed
into being. Powered with the instincts of strays,

your dogs stay clear. Palms glowing,
backs chilled, we rotate around the crimson axis
whose blooms unfurl, throwing sparks,

falling back quicker than a heart's trepidation
about yet another year swallowed whole,
leaving its souvenirs: dregs, smoky clothes,
news rolled up and gone to ashes.

We too are strays within darkness.
Here in the East, time is split and shared.
In the West, cured alone too long for its salt.

Already it's time to move back to the blue
droughts, silences smooth as the roads. Already
the minutes tick inside buttery laburnum buds,

mynahs swell with eggs and a climbing sun
matures the bumpy skin of custard apples.
There's no knowing the best way to squeeze
through a crack in the taxi door parked

too close to a wall, to step away and board
a jumbo jet winding up slow as a kept resolution.
Shrill for the whole thousand-mile song.

VICTORY FOR THE ANCESTORS

One of the warriors holds a dove, another ties a well-oiled string
to its foot. In a world of one-hundred-and-ten-degree heat,
duty is a line between eye and gut pulled so taut it can vault
over ramparts without a thought of all they have left
behind: wife, mother, compassion. It is time to light up a string

tied to one dove. Another. A dozen strings, each tied to a foot,
are lit. The lion-breath heat is intense. Only the thorny acacias
offer shade from air now a-shimmer with gray and white wings.
Each dove chased home by a steady flame that licks its way
up a length, toward the feet and tail feathers.

The emperor who rode down from the Himalayas, through
the great plains, made all drop to their knees. A trail of music,
ice, designs for inlays of garnet and lapis lazuli, followed him.
Thousands of ovals polished and sharpened. Knife-like edges

set flush in palace walls of marble. One signal from him and ranks
lined up, traveled miles. Now the warriors' eyes follow flight's arc
where the doves are disappearing behind fortress walls
so heavily guarded approach has been impossible for weeks.

Smoke curls up from the fort's eaves. Shouts rise from within.
A great door creaks open. Soldiers, princes, queens
burst out ahead of their rebel king. He is riding his blue horse.
Sunlight sharpens the day into a thousand arrows.

A seventeenth-century emperor gives the orders,
and the ancestors have to obey.

CALLING FROM ACROSS CONTINENTS

On the other side of the world, I hold on while you rise
from your phone in a subcontinent of gutted biographies
where raw light seeps through hours of half-sleep
spent cringing on the outskirts of fire. An eerie presence,
a dictator's shrilling entering the radio waves.
The morning seems normal. A koel's warble, a bicycle bell,
the newspaper recycler's yodel. Now the faint flare
and fall of voices exchanging notes while you pay
the house-to-house vendor for vegetables bought
the day before. My other tongue stirring awake
from a time when it hid behind sandstone and rubble,
dashed for the cover of a rickety table. Your receipt folded
over and over to fit under the leg and calm the shaking.

How we held still, one floor above the chaos. The old fort
not quite in ruins. Below us, hordes blood-eyed with smoke
and belligerent readiness rushing the streets. The cans
of petrol, the matches. Minds lit by a leader on a motorcycle.
A hit list clouding his rearview mirror, his vision of a future
released from curfew. None looked up. We were still,
the minutes backing away from heat so thick that sweat
and oils rose to dissolve words before they were spoken.
Walls collapsed between faces of fire. Smoke filled the view
for all but one moment, a tiny mass swaying high at the tip
of a pitchfork. Unborn fetus the color of sliced pomegranate.
There was no before, no after. Each of us caught at the edge
of a spinning center. Now you return to the phone.
Our talk circles the aftermath without touching it.

In 1984, riots and fires broke out across the city of Delhi
after Prime Minister Indira Gandhi was assassinated.

BLACKBIRDS IN A BARE TREE AT DUSK

Their trills are part praise,
                part concern about the mundane:
        proteins, plummeting temperatures.
                The roiling gray weather to come
is detected by clavicle and dampness of feather.
        The whole tree has turned into a brain
        powered by voices, metallic calls and responses
connecting the dots, the branched dendrons and ganglia
        of their minds, like a cluster of festival lights
        blinking with ideas, reiterating the boon
                of collective consciousness.
The birds are aware of the increasing lack of light
        and leaf, roosting branches
                that will drop all but the skeletal.
Hardwired to seasonality, the chorus floats up
                one voice seconds another, a third,
an anthem longing for countries saturated with sun.
        One mind, nerves in coordination,
                knows to rub the heat back
        into its ruffled parts, cling to the good air
                between feather and down. By the time
        the sky is replete with the hydrogen
                and hematite of burning stars,
                        each bird will be ready for a silence
        that fires up its cells.
                In the language of rocks, every inch
                        represents ten thousand years.
        In the language of birds, every feather, bone.

OF THE FORESTS AFTER FIRE

THE SIERRA: A HISTORY

Not long after lightning has rushed down the electric staircase of its own making, not long after fires five stories tall have swept up-canyon, a new season the size of pearls begins. Silences spreading like hands to touch the heads of seedling and fiddlehead nudging out by the hundreds through ceilings of soil and ashy debris. Hours as loose as scree firming up in tender grips.

Here a stand of charred oaks unwraps its storage of gangly leaves, there a knot of cones thrown open by heat releases seeds ripe for sun. Currents of brightness are charged from within. Sunlight plucks at the strings of top branches. Up at the crown, blackened firs begin again their story of vigor, edged with new needles. The irresistible music, tinsel-and-chime notes. Wind nosing close to the buds to receive all the answers.

The burned and crackling world not in shambles. Not gone to ash and ash alone. Sapsucker, pileated, black-backed woodpeckers, all join the jig of genetic diversity. All build from scratch. What do they crave? Riches. Riches hidden in the wide-open arches rising from gray.

Many of the trees that initially look dead are not. —Chad Hanson

DIABLO WINDS

We woke to shrill voices and smoke.
Winds letting go; messages flying far.
A pine-and-cedar incense of imminence
wrapping the stars. *Santa Ana, Diablo, Fohn.*
Pages flapping. Nothing to hold the books,
the photos, the shared cups of tea, to the moment.
Rooms loosened from meaning. Walls
turning into paper in the hands of chance.
Anything, anything, grabbed without thought.
The mind a leaf spinning. The prayers caught
in our throats for months. One for shelter,
one for first responders knocking on doors.
One for the lost, one for fighters driving through flames.
One for the hills rimmed with a rolling brightness,
for history to make us wise about lands
that have always returned after fire. For time, for time.
For the surprises tiptoeing in, unannounced, just weeks
after the flames. One for rain and the rise of suncup,
biscuitroot, toadflax and whispering bells.
For the plentiful flaring open, petals upon ash,
songbirds upon branches of charcoal,
black bear upon berries of abundance, fresh juices
trickling down the corners of her mouth.

A very powerful force of nature that's been here for millions of years.
Will be here for millions more. —Tim Ingalsbee

REJUVENATION

Once we have looked away, once we have mourned
and banished all smoldering thoughts about the tribe
of blackened trees replacing the known world—
for now and another season—and the last long fingers
of smoke have been ushered out by wind, a ticking begins.
No one has seen them arriving in such numbers, but the birds
are neither lost nor passing through. They are simply linked
tight to the newborn scents of ash and rain, to the promise
of white fruits, the riches concealed by bark.

So were the ways of ancestors who began their journeys as
specks in the distance, some fifty thousand years ago. Riding
the miles of smoky gold, along a known line of hunger,
growing closer and closer. The rufous beat of instinct working
a migration upstream, against the flow of smoke, into the
source and its multiple treasures.

One new arrival looks bright with hope. He preens his dusk-
and-opal plumage. Others tap as if knocking on doors. The
answers have been provided by the ages, delicate as genetic
fibers coiled in every cell—beak and bone, muscle and shiny
eye. The living are awake to the profusion soon to follow.
They will grow with the diligence of all known colors
unfurling from the soil's chocolatey darkness, from the trees
re-greening come spring, from the blackness.

That burned tree—it's the legacy, it's the beginning.
—Dominick DellaSala

GIGANTEUM, THE REDWOOD

To think of you as miles of you. Much more
than the lone colossus guarding a bare canyon
bereft of the rest. As the receiver of skies
streaked with soliloquy, runlets seeping down
crypts of time and slopes steeped in peelings.
As the giant amidst a history of giants sipping
waters pooling in great goblets of basalt below
ground, poised on a subterranean table wider
than a city. To think of you as story unuttered,
as stowage of time anchored by root claw.
As clarity filtered, light chutes angling in to
be chopped into slivers and photons. Eaten.
As the growth of built sugars—cone, trunk,
dragon-tailed branch—amassed from sunlight
and carbon dioxide. As verticals gathering
spotted owls and rain dripping over curtains
of insects hovering close. To comprehend
your gravity and single status as hope beyond
remnant. As assemblage, shadows many
stories tall, cooling wet gravel. As Amazons
in conference, recalling silences before Miwok
fires, metal, flight. As axioms of the vertical
world's slow spinning.

TRANSLATION IN FIRST LIGHT

Knowing you were gone for good, I walked
to where hallways of pine led to fog.
Crept under barbed wire and on across
the swale's soaked grasses, shoulder to shoulder
with spikerush, *Juncus*. Tips burnt to ocher

by a season of sinking back
as if seed send-off was fire, a sun-pinched end.
As if coupling itself had torched them open.
I thought to reach past the winking drifts,
the unanchored cobwebs. To fall back
on the reliable densities: dogwood, red willow.

Blade of grass on my tongue—from squirming
under the fencing? A burnt trunk still alive,
green at the base and crown, gave a bit
to my leaning. I wanted to reread your note,
the writing sloping downward, the weight
that could not be pulled out of darkness.

But my hands were silt-caked, knees drenched
in crushed dewdrops, mud, from ducking
and kneeling under the wandering threads of loss—
all silk, all drive, without a spot to fasten on.

Then the sun flooded in, the air cleared.
And a lone sparrow caterwauled her lamentations
from behind shifting screens. *Kis-ki-dee, kis-ki-dee,*
proclaiming the world rejuvenated,
my back-pocket pages rendered with rhythm.
And there was no need to reopen.

NOW YOU CAN SET DOWN YOUR FEARS

A sweep of brightness raises the mountaintops from sleep.
As if on cue, a rush of breath answers the stuff of ages,
the essentials, lands and gurgling waters awakened
by silences rising once the flames have fallen.

Now you can set down your fears. You can see
the tribes arriving. Sprig by sprig, the forests
unwrapping layers of light. The old and the new, shoulder
to shoulder. Ambers, reds, and greens, following

internal instructions. Lily, lupine, conifer, marking time
in concentric circles, working through their intricacies.
Now the wild ones, with inner eyes drawing
from the Pleistocene, are arriving with the disposition

of their ancients. And the order. Mice, owls, foxes yipping.
Lines of pilgrims with the training, the shape and scents
of paths mapped out. And now the mule deer, the lions.
All along, they knew to arrive. To shift and settle into place,
in a vast machinery of rebirth—tasting the good light,

anticipating the soot on their feet, the unknowns. Listening
for scratchy sounds. A trilling laces the bite of air. Winks of light
catch a tiny pool of dew held in a swordfern's hollow.
All the looseness of soil, potash, charcoal, crumbly

between the press of finger and thumb, is firming up
in grip-shaped roots steadily descending into darkness.
The air still, the breath of seedlings edging out
of slumber. Close to the treetops, inches of relearning

find their way out of the shadows. New whorls echo
the shape of their burned predecessors. Faith alights
on the sooty drapes covering trees. The birds cling, flash.
Announce the sap, the squirming meats, the great bounty.

COYOTE

Sun on grass exhales the downpour of seconds ago. Coyote comes trotting through the steam, across the field alive with glitter. Unrushed, carving a wide arc around necessity. Eyes and belly keen. Now stops, quick-sinking to a crouch. Ears forward, picking up a scratchy fidgeting. The gopher's whole body—mouth, nose, eyes—shoveling dirt from its shallow cave. Coyote grows tense. The fudge-brown body surfaces. Jaws clamp down, toss. The prey stands toothy and defiant, ready to fight. Coyote whines. Lunges and grips it again, tenderly, as if tweaking an error. Another toss and recapture, a third, a fourth. Behind them the orchestra of greens is fading. Now the gopher falls without defiance or teeth, no more than a floppy toy, lost atop its maze of tunnels. The fur will turn into soil; the soil will surge up as grass. The sound of crunching is so faint it could be the wind itself, crackling and snapping.

SMOKE-DETECTING BEETLES

In answer to drifts of ash, to genetic unity, a current soars
up and west. Clouds of longhorns, yellow-velvets, fir sawyers.
Barely able to wait till the ashes cool, till the crackling
lowers to a murmur of embers. Wings shimmer across

the air thermals. A hundred miles of ridgeline and vale,
a hundred more, the unheard music of migration.
The fire-brushed lands call to them with refrains that took shape
when the first trees were torched open by lightning

millions of years ago. The refrains beckon. Smoke-drifts
and haze by day, fission-eyes of stellar matter arranged
like a cambered map by night. And the beetles yield.
Charged with hybrids of black and gold, their wings are blurred
with a flight that is so much about turbulence and fury,

about mind over wind, that it is less insects in flight
than the hurrying of a black-veined river, less a wing-beaten
composite of airborne probabilities than electric gale, less
mass migration than an a cappella more ancient than decision.

CLINGSTONE

Time to pluck the peaches, the plums. Top ones warmest to the touch. Fan out your shirt for a basket we can fill. With hurry, your hair rinsing my face. With journeys, the morning my cherry-red train puffed and you ran along the platform, waving—one hand gripping the window railing that smelled of rain. Fingertips touching, letter to letter, for weeks. Time now, to reach for the top branches, the sweetmeats ready to give. The world swings, the shift of leafy shadows over stone is swift. What small fires we hold. Pressed fruit gives easily— two halves of a whole—juices bursting in the moment's mouth to fill past absences, uncertainties. Tree frogs tick all around, vocal sacs bubbling. Click by click, our picking straightens the bowing branches. Abundance is as tender as hope. Clingstones are saved in pockets. Stained cloth, drunken bees, the susurrus of hands splashing through red-tinged leaves.

Days swell.
The starfruit sun
seasons time.

PILEATED HOMEMAKER

My neighbor is building a new home.
No note or preamble preceded the *rap-*
rap-rap, insisting my eardrums report
the vitality of his presence well before six
this morning. He must come from a land
of early risers, where only the owners
who claim their corner of dawn may keep it.
I could deliver lemonade, hint that
his acreage will remain his at eleven or noon.
Outside, the wood chips fly, firing up
before they plummet from the sun. The hammer
bellowing a hollow into its wooden pole
is his beak. Claws clench. The scarlet cap of feathers
unruffled though he pounds with bony fortitude.

Surely the repercussions of such steady staccatos
could be grave. Nights, I keep windows sealed,
fans near for white noise that gives sleep
a chance to glide past the first crack. He's still there.
I pace my days with Mozart, Chopin, Schumann
played loud enough so the background *rat-a-tat*
roughly compares with the crackle of dust
encountering my needle as each LP races 'round
and 'round in an endless quest for beauty.
Once I emerge and a flash of raven-like wings
is quickly lost to depths of forest.

The weeks of drilling and beveling are over.
Solos of longing echo across the valley. Not echoes—
someone is calling back. She has flown in
to test the oval foyer, to crawl in, clucking.
Their beaks touch. He delivers a wood-worm.

MOUNTAIN QUAIL

On the far side of absence, a clean drop,
a mist-driven dawn. One quail foraging
where there have always been two.
A lean season, air spiced with the chopped
and fallen bark of fir and cedar. Her chest is afire

with agitation. I too straighten my neck
for the encounter. In the pause, she scratches
the dirt, the maw left by bulldozers, and pecks.
Persistence is the strongest of fruits.
Even the whole, halved, seeks to function

as whole. Even after their hold
lies loosened, roots dangling askew,
leaves continue their drive through the murk
drawing from fists entrenched in clay. The quail
is surrounded by a swirling, a white-outed cliff

below. Generations of wisdom have equipped her
to perceive my prolonged attention as a threat.
The moment flees into the unthinkable.
I cannot help bushwhacking towards the drop.
Leaning over the sheer face of absence,

pulling sticks and leaves from my hair.
Far below, she is clinging to the edge of life—
the way we all do. The scratches stinging
my face and arms, too, will all but vanish.

FUNGAL CRUMBLE

Picture consuming the forest's detritus whole.
Mushroom heads and miles of subterranean fuzz
hover and touch the goods. Toothless mouths
growing full of ripe juices, the discarded,
the ground-down. And the crunchy ones, the charred,
the shadow-soft flooring of needles. All taken

one bite at a time. The quiet voyage from cast-offs
to soil begins with pressure less than an eyelash,
weight slighter than sunlight on skin.
Enzymes make mean heat. Their mode is cloak
and dagger, liquid teeth, underground feet.
Their chemistry tangos with moisture and scat,

with crunch of elk foot and moon-opened throat
of coyote. In the silence that follows,
our saprophytes raise thin goblets of mud tea
and suck out the innards of soft-boiled seeds
with fluids and minuscule straw. In a month
of mornings, the standing dead will be covered

in a gauzy web. Seasons from now, their remains
will crumble to nub and hunch. Cakey soils made
from the quiet digestions. Fungal spores will float
off the dense mass without fuss,
like wandering moons hunting the ridgelines
of resistance, the valleys of give. Always
at the ready to recycle, to raze the dead.

BAND-TAILED PIGEONS AFTER THE STORM

Lightning all night,
    leaves smacking and chattering around
      the flock. Nothing but wetness to cling to.
Eyes shut tight against
    the momentary tongues of brilliance,
    Flickers of dread are muted
by dreams thin as gauze,
    mitigating the bellow of thunder.
Resilience is single-minded,
bowed heads braving the air currents
    roaring and hurling sheets of water.
      Now rain-grays rinse the half-sun.
    The flock lifts, opening the sky.
Their soto voce is one voice, their thoughts
one thought. To circle the sub-cloud altitudes,
    arranging and rearranging the light.
Their minds emptied of everything else.
    Mass movement has one purpose,
    one ethos, no room for dispute.
When the thick chains of sunlight
drop their gold, the flock spirals down.
    Swish of arrival echoing through leaves,
a shower of droplets shaken loose.

DEFORESTATION

By evening the mountains are women
wrapped in dark shawls. They sit hunched
over embers. The quiet exchange spans
the ages, the present. The living know
less, or nothing. We are restless as wind
streaking the sky with cirrus and smoke.
We are no more than a moment of phoebes
and bluebirds rising and falling to their thin,
plaintive ribbons of sound. The path ahead

is a lantern of minutes sputtering out. Smells
of resin and freshly slashed cedar stain
the end of days. If only our miles were not
drained by battle, all hopes of listening gone
to marauders, the briefest of petals falling
through our hands. What will we say
to the coming generations, sun slipping down

with all our time, aches starting to show cracks
that widen as landslides. Night grasses
flattening under the blood of runoff. Rivers
losing silver tongues to erosion. The world
liquefied, racing down. Few left to call it home.

YUBA RIVER

Blue of a billion years blasting ravines into being.
Blue the power of infinity beginning with sand grain.
Simple to return to the stillness of blue.
Undercurrents holding and releasing
the substrates, surfaces rich in flashing silver.
Silk-blue irises tasting the spray and light.
Ribbons of time salmoning upstream
through waterfalls. Blue memory
of a snapped string of pearls sliding down
my neck. Gone like their giver. Blue of a bruise,
cause unknown. Blue the vast depths below
tending toward darkness, hollows
of shadowy caves translucent as jelly.
Underneath the blues are dollops of life:
motionless frogs so spotted by the ages
they blend with the backdrop of stones.
Blue of the heart's staccatos of relief
watching waters set free. Light a blue flame
for coffee while dawn's tongue dissolves stars
like sugar. Blue to the power of blue,
and none of it enough.

CLOAKS OF CHARCOAL

The burned trees are gathered by the hundreds. Each cloak of charcoal a sooty ship-mast floating upright in a sea of new leaves and thick slices of earth. All around are expanses of cedar, fir, and pine, blackened from their base to eye level, alive. Dawn brings a busy uproar—wrens, bluebirds, black-backed woodpeckers, lazuli buntings, pygmy nuthatches, and red-breasted sapsuckers. The first touch of sun clings to tree-tops like honey. A child is bending to pick miner's lettuce. Her father has found morels by Two-Mile Creek. Hope that was tough as heat-cracked rocks grows soft, buoyant, as leaves fluorescing from half-burned trees.

The land holds all—a mosaic of fiery intensities, showers of ash on floors heaped with debris. The land's memory becomes its healing, its secrets, its breads, butters, and preserves released. The child has found herself among monkeyflowers, shooting stars, clarkias and solitary bees, constellations of seedlings stretching out from decades of sleep. She listens to mountain quails calling attention to the riches. She sees leavings, prints where bear and deer foraged.

The walking animals have known for millennia, the insects for longer. Smoke runs through their instincts like greetings in a familiar language. Rivers of birds have always been riding in on the rivers of insects that swarmed towards the source; the salts of burned branches have always been sinking, slow-melting in rain. The larvae chew their way through woody tunnels. Foxes and ringtail cats switch from perch to perch. Now the child too is singing.

Western forests have evolved with mixed-severity fires, and new trees naturally grow back on their own . . . —Doug Bevington

ONE BANYAN TREE BECOMES A FOREST

All summer long, the hanging strands
tribe, a loosened braid. Gateways guiding
not all possess the vector, the piercing
precision will ground, spark up as leaf.
distance   down to zero—to renew
and hurry are unknowns. Only a slow all,
air. A beginning. Aims plumb as intuition,
them. An obstinacy of lignin, knowing no
itself. A craving for root, hair, straw, the
not gravitational pull that directs.
exploration apart from dirt crumb, hope
from worm or leafy debris. As if the tonnage
be tied down a hundred times over to prevent
plunging,   arrival   treasured.   The
Mississippi, Orinoco—all teach the same. Skin
of darkness gaining hold. Sprouting. Proliferation
swallowing salts and blue speeches of water.
as patience, a festival as the radiance of eventuals.
buds, as obedience yearning for a knot. Body falls,
a script of green sun.   To pluralize.

reaching for earth. All of a
from air to earth, though
whose nail-in-leather
Few with the forte to narrow
breathing. Acceleration
an island of scribbles in
and nothing to stop
shelter from gale but
minuscule sipping. It's
It's faith, an inability to tell
from night, rising dream
of monastery must
flight. Leap of faith
ancients—Ganges,
of fire and body
by means of
An inch a season
Aims meek as
falls, to rise up

RECITATION FOR AN ASH-SCATTERING CEREMONY

darkness roaring from beyond the great groves
coming up to my knees   hips   now shoulders
the urn full of her ashes carried away in the flow
will continue to carry me
along the trajectory of evening walks   gentler

than a hair's touch   her hand at the back of my neck
not so much pressure   as pulling away
a way of sequestering the knowledge of her own
upcoming disappearance   light all around
gradually blowing color into the intricacies of bark
and heart-shaped leaves   rising in pairs on pale wings

there is   within the forests we breathe
an ancient manner   spurred into being
by lightning   the oaks and red firs splitting at the helm
driving themselves into sleep   willing
all known treasures to the coming generations

seed heads unclasped, the cracking open of shells
whose journeys into being were always fire
and are here to shape us and our slight shadows
following in their footsteps   we who are infants
too young on this earth to gauge the impacts
of blade and heavy tread   too quick to listen
while saplings rise   like a carpet of sparks
we the latecomers   not pausing to ask

not waiting for the seasons following ash
where the tops of blackened trees flush
layers of morning spilling brilliance
and the newness drawing flocks

like blown embers   and the raptors
luminous   all here long before memory
and here now to wake us

For Gouri Khosla

ELEGY FOR THE MISSING

The birds will neither be found nor
buried. Songs will be replaced by the
thunderous slam of legacies. Once in
a while, a crack along a mid-section
of trunk will reveal a home, a bulbous
cave carved deep in pulp, surfaces
pecked and beveled with precision.
The ones who lived here: woodpecker,
wren, pygmy owl. All are nameless. It
is not fire that extinguishes. It is the
churning of seasons, noise and slash,
truckloads carrying the remains away.
We are nomads circling the edges.
A lone olive-sided flycatcher sings vespers. Corridors, hallways
of trees, lost to dusk and loose soil. By night, candles sinking to
their knees. Outpourings congealing to white on a stump. The
bulldozers gone, the silences stinging our faces with salt and blown
dust. Organized disappearance looks simple, clean. The shape
of the missing hunched between us. Our hands empty, racing
like water over our tasks. No time for rituals to commemorate.
We crave the ones who cannot be
shown the way home. We will not
look authority in the eye, or say
much if we do. But the fallen, whose
gutted   remains   are   tapped
by ravens, will leave voices behind.
Will become semaphores. We will
walk across shadeless miles, paying
our last respects. The curious who
follow will grow. Chants will surge
through the multitudes, across the
good country, sealing these lines.

Trees logged in the years after fire are full of nests.

AS IF WE HAD TIME

WIND TURBINE HITS THE HAWK

Is this the way we fail time—racing in place
a vortex overpowering flight, taking measures
of vitality for itself, the infinite air, the spinning.
Standing behind parted grasses, she is just shy of two feet
tall. Left wing sloped at an odd angle. The crest feathers
find strength to rise against my presence, beak and eye

widening, silent fury. One backwards hop reveals the drag,
the snapped shoulder. The burning senescence quickened
by bacteria crowding into the wound, micron-sized flies
eager to work blood into rust. The soundless buzz
of degradation sapping light from her eyes. Pain is private.
The minutes will turn into months of wondering

if it was right to spread my jacket wide, to drop it
over her. Claws prepared to lacerate the silence went still.
As I walked the great curve of grassland she was weightless,
not substantial enough for her name, *Buteo jamaicensis*.
A weightless bundle transferred into a cardboard box, with holes
poked through for air. The drive to the rescue center

was full of sky. Blues blazing on and off between trees,
a daydream of the raptor taking wing. She was a shadow
rising to power the updrafts. Gazing down on filigrees
of grass and burrows below, the ultraviolet ribbons
of mouse urine, the twitching, hurried maneuvers—
which looked utterly futile from her bird's eye view.

THE BALANCE OF ICE AND AIR

Sea lion pups beach out of season. Sky's wine
and coral flames press down on arctic nights
thickening with salty heat. The balance of ice
and light is tipped, spilling into sea. Turtle embryos
turn from male to female in the hot confines

of their eggs. Percentages climb beyond history,
the carbon dioxide meter in Mauna Loa rising to 350,
400, 405. Seconds before touchdown, summer rains
shatter into virga, arrows the opposite of falling.
A cactus's long-held barrel of water runs low. I hold

a surf-perch and she lets go, six slimy newborns
wriggling in my hand. The good sun stabs through
underwater ribbons. This moment is all. Prehistoric bubbles
of ice bursting through isinglass waters. Light firing up
the understory. Permafrost made temporary,

rain-soaked glitterings of salmon-berry crisping
on the vine. Unfathomable as denial and devoid of air.
Mud-mired ice clicks in metamorphosis.
Out beyond the tide's musculature, the sea lion parents
graze on weedy remains. The pups are stranded,

an unknown gravity greater than hunger binding them
to the shoreline. Bedraggled children know no more
than to stare into the source of collapse. Between them
a great blue drum of hope dragged in. Rotating
around its axis, unstoppable.

> *A laboratory in Mauna Loa, Hawaii, has been monitoring a steady rise
> in carbon dioxide, an agent of climate change.*

FROM THE ASH BEDS

The blossoms ignite their silks with rainwater
sucked from the earth, petals afire with light.
Wallflower, manzanita, dogwood.
All fall open, unguarded, eager to blaze,
eager to embark on the long dream of release
shining with the desire to consume
daylight. To take the long trip towards fruit
and dispersal, towards futures shaped by the pull
of sun. Each spares no expense in its rush

to further passage, swelling towards generations
ahead, pollen tongues and ovaries advancing
in chemical silence. Like a window, caged pigeons,
or anything framed by its limits, each petal flares
to the edges of its niche, spends all its light
before crinkling up like a used ticket.

But little is lost. The seeds send out their musk. Deer
and flying squirrels draw close, nose past the fallen petals
and nibble the fruits. The stones come of age inside
their foragers' guts. Sealed and safe, they ride
through valleys in darkness growing ready,
ready to become emissaries of the past, coded for color,
sex, and the abundance of summers yet to arrive.
Ready to carpet their future refuge with precision
—sight unseen.

CACTUS IN SPRING

Stillness is power, thick as a tree-trunk. Holding
    fluids and every permutation of what it takes to wait,
  while the air heaves weights of clouds
that will not give. Finally, the deluge arrives, descending
    with such force, the top-soil can neither hold
nor translate. Runlets swallowing tumbleweeds,
    packrat homes, clumps of earth,
        on their boiling journey nowhere.
Rapid-fire flows that couldn't possibly quench the living.
Or so it seems. Yet here's the upshot: prickly densities
crowned with mother-of-pearl petals steeped in sweetness
moths and hummingbirds spinning
  around the succulence
        like dizzy satellites.
Cactuses stand apart and leave to chance
    the mute hurry for union and sticky closure.
   Blooms are crammed to the core
with white riches, male dust brought in by moth feet,
antennae, bird beaks.
  One brush of dust against female glue turns all to bliss.
      Underworlds of ovaries and oil-tipped pollen
    swell as seeds. Petals shrivel. The wind's briefest breath
    scatters them across the sand.

SEA TURTLES ARRIVE

Desire and good timing are tangled forever in darkness.
     All who emerge are the offspring of an edge
          whose salts and sighs echo those of the waves.
We who have traveled hundreds of miles stand back,
     the night rising and sinking under phosphorescence
               churned up by the crash
          and back-sizzle of sand.
There is a map of cool green light
          giving mystery a chance to surface and breathe,
and swell to the shape of a stranger. A thousand strangers,
          more. Each of them heaped with eggs
     and expectations. The immense surge of instinct
makes them forget the dangers, the coming of light.
               No choice but to sink to our knees in sand
terrified that life, laden with plum-sized pearls of the future,
               could lose her lumbering grip on this world.
     And though the egg-encumbered turtles
          cannot afford to care about the perils of a painful crawl,
     evolution does. And has created this crazed saturation—
          we could walk on their shells for miles,
     never once treading on sand.
          Persistence has no choice but itself,
     older than the Jurassic moment
          the females began embarking
          on this flipper-footed scraping,
this egg-laying struggle, eyelids shutting and opening,
          eyes full of tear-gel gazing seaward.

THE SPONTANEOUS FIRE OF TOXINS

Beware, bellows the sign. But the fawn
is already stepping past the rim of plastic.
Fore-hoofs and knees in the pond. Neck bent,
the lips touch and the head jerks back.

Once I wanted to expose the secrets
dissolved in water, but the days
spun out of reach, assessments scattering
like so many papers in the wind.

Phosphine burned
with search-light brilliance, glittering
under eyelids long after sleep.

The fawn bolts towards dry brush,
stamping hard,
mouth and fore-hooves are on fire.
Droplets shake loose, ignite in air

twist into nothings of smoke.
Listen—blood is immense
I heard that pounding
and opened the forest's door.

Silence and the metrics of absence
swooping in. Smoke smelling of hide,
the world spinning without word.

Flames strip trust.
Smoldering twigs snap and flatten
under the fawn's shaky jumps.

Listen. You can hear the pounding
of a double-beating heart.
attempting to turn away, to breathe.

HURT

My day's labor: relocating the living. I long for
the end. Bulldozers level the good savannah, the O
of burrows. Grassy susurrations hushed. Homes
of snake, salamander, frog, compacted. Plovers
alight between water trucks and unearthed nothings,

jabbing at rhizomes and worms. Now a shimmering
bicycle tire is no longer a tire. *Need gloves?*
The foreman waves, gestures me through a gathering
circle. Men switching off their dinosaur engines,
leaping out. Thicker than a wrist, the king snake

writhes around a flattened part of its six-foot form,
bands of cream and pitch-black. Smears of dusty blood
showing through. Lifted, he offers mild ripples
of resistance, radial muscles writhing in waves inching

further and further from grip. His weight is an ache
in my arms. The willows and shade look far.
He turns into a standing wave. The poise of a Shiva
holds his body, the forked tongue, testing for shelter
where I set him down. The job done, terror and elation

take hold of the understory. Sweat tightens my hardhat.
Pungent scents on my clothes. How often love walks
the perimeter of apocalypse, passing the trash and riprap.
How easy to mistake the alternating bands of light and dark
for signs of hope.

HALF A SENTENCE

You left mid-sentence. I tried everything to stop
rain's echo, a second shower, willow leaves.
Before the pyre I took shooting star earrings from your lobes.
O waning moon, you scattered the clouds.

Rain's echo, a second shower, willow leaves
shimmering like silk saris shot through with silver.
O waning moon, you scattered the clouds
a dance that continues after the drumming has ceased

to glimmer like silk saris shot through with silver.
Still, you live in bird glitter, in the willow's spring brio,
a dance that continues after the drumming has departed
from the rose silk fin of morning, green silk fin of day.

Stay close to water. Come near, dove-foot girl—
You left mid-sentence. I tried everything to stop
bud jasmine, jamun flowers from being placed in your hair
before the pyre I took shooting star earrings from your lobes.

For Tilottama Basu

CRASH OF RHINOS

You who shudder the flies off your backs are few, blended in with mud and silt. You may vanish long before your time. You may vanish in the name of the so-called aphrodisiac lining the white of your keratin. Already the world is falling to stochastic shifts in temperature. Already your absences are greater than the meadow-rich expanses shepherding your origins, guiding your young. A sky's wheel of gulls crying about the circle of vultures below. Many among you cannot help straying across the river that usurps your floodplain every few seasons. Horns are sliced off by poachers avid for more. Their knife-edge hands. Your crash with its volume turned off. Scents of blood and ribcage draw civet and fishing cat. Hooves and skin-shields sink beyond view. Remains pass on to the larger family—hyenas, then fungus. Glassy plates of surface tension fold and buckle. Wind enters the crumpled water, emerges as an incantation tinctured with cartilage. Forks of purpled light flash before slipping from the sky like nameless fish. The rest is for beauty to cover the drag marks, the time-diminished chaos, as beauty is inclined to do. Bunchgrass, acacia, the crowns of great trees eventually touching above the spot where one of you gave birth, nuzzled the soft fragment of time.

RIOT

The woman unfastens the pins and her hair tumbles
down her sari, back-lit by dusk. A long mirror
doubles the light. Oiling and combing,
she inspects herself, the dying sky. A haziness
creeping in, staining it. The front gate creaks open.
Fingers shake as she bends double, reaches for slippers.
Slight feet flutter down. She fills a steel tumbler
with iced water, droplets beading along the sides.
Closes the front door behind her, water in hand.
The man is wide-eyed, barefooted, top three buttons
and collar ripped from his shirt. He drains the tumbler.
She can smell his burned hair, the violence watched
by the mob who inflicted it. Trickles run down
his blistered neck. *More will walk this way.*
What she smells could be cooking-fire smoke,
but for its rubbery thickness. And the birds gone
silent too early. All night she will sit outside, dipping
into a vessel. Tumbler after tumbler will be offered.
All night, her dreams will roar from the other side
of time where the destitute materialize
from lamp-lit streets, bodies limp as flags
yearning for their anthem. One by one they will bow,
cupping their hands in darkness, drinking as she pours.
The mobs will close in, molten as stars.

For R. Thapar

CANCER

Winds sweetened, an overcast sky bulged
low enough to give. It did not give. Not even
the thinnest gesture, drizzle. My mother turned
back, pretending the view had pleased her,

licked a forefinger, straightened a parched crease
in my blouse. Feigning contentment, I filled time.
Buckets and bowls brimming with sunlight
before the faucet water ran out at nine.

Medicinal roots were boiled, a luke-warm tub filled,
bougainvillea petals sprinkled. Blouses and skirts
steam-pressed under an iron whose belly was loaded,
live coals hissing with heat nothing could soften.

Leafing through the crackle-dry pages of a volume
sulfured by time and silver bugs, we found songs
about fish dancing on their ears in rice fields flooded
with rain and riches. Now my mother was singing,

beckoning the clouds for monsoon rains
to cure a peculiar thirst tied up in knots.
Searching the mirror more than she searched the sky.
Testing her strength with leafy strands of hope.

Then the afternoon sun draped clouds
with shifting silks, like two women exchanging gifts
of red rice and scarves, before parting ways
for a journey they knew only one could take.

FOG ODE

River without weight, without sound. Serpent,
canyon-ghost, valley-to-valley rider, brushstroke

slighter than hair across the face of pre-light.
Fluids that float until caught on twig, land-cloud

never diminished for all the dripping that fills
underground pools with the abundance of summer

drinks for redwood, dogwood, sorrel, and fir.
Mist-breath, winged current, whitest of air

barely present but for mild subtractions of color—
oak minus depth of green, dawn minus blush,

brick minus dusty puce. River of minutes, giver
without gravity, silence in a cloak, listening without an ear.

Memory of the Mississippi, the Eel, the Orinoco,
more than enough, yet vanishing when sundried.

Voiceless sweet-water sweeping past needle-tip,
thorn-tip, rim of leaf. Edges poised to catch a million

mist-drops. Gauzy sleeve caught against branch
or stem, trickling down hollows to pools too dim

to reflect the nimbleness of their source.
Cleanser, sun-scatterer, quilt-but-not-quilt. Recaller

of streams long past, maker of forests
within forests, builder of cathedral-groves,

taker of nothing but morning sun, no one
could fathom what you are worth.

A POET'S KEYSTONE

Cool to the palm, easy to lose, it is everywhere.
Spherical as song bubbles surfacing

from a winter wren's depth among dogwoods.
Familiar as the ache of turtles ready to hatch

with the force of egg-tooth and newborn fluids.
Guarded by fish-hook cacti defending

their jelly-globes with pointed gestures.
Described by the ball-and-socket joints

of an ibex carcass, dropped and dashed to pieces
by lammergeier vultures diving down for the marrow.

Shaken inside the rattling cup of a beggar's child.
Sweet under the skin of wild cucumbers crowned

with thorns, hidden in the night-dark gnarl of tree rot
visited by the slant of sun just once a year.

Contained in a loose assemblage of cobble
cupping a fire's face in canyons of sandstone

that face the late light. Housed in the same shelters
that lengthened the dance of ancestor hands

along walls of firelight and shadow.
Spoken in the voice of mid-river boulders

grinding in flood. Glorified by the ebbing flow
the silence smooth and round as stone.

GIRLS WANDERING THROUGH
A MUSTARD FIELD

Plunging into the cloud of button blooms, they vanish.
Swish of clothes against Brassica. The giddiness,
the freedom. Four-petal suns the size of fingernails
festooning cheeks and arms with pollen. Encounters

that bring on a trembling elation, a thrill, contained
in nervous hesitation. A rushing forward paired
with a pulling back, each one's hands clinging
to another's arm or scarf. The leader's careful steps.

The one behind, slipperless on the cracked earth.
The percussive slap of feet. Then the shy one,
the graceful one, with a star of leucoderma
across her neck. Only the wake of arms
doing breast-strokes through the golden cloud,

pressing stems aside, is visible. Each second is rinsed
by the need to venture beyond the lasso of adult voices
ready to order them back. But not yet, not yet.
Now they glide through the tunneled secrets
of bitter honey, blooms that will soon relinquish

their hold on gold, morph into seed. Each girl will grow
used to forced absences from home, to averting
her veiled face from mustard seeds spattering
in a skillet of oil. To the slow back-burn of fate.

The sati student was taught the virtues of immolating herself
on her husband's funeral pyre. The schools were outlawed.

SEA TURTLE HATCHLINGS HEADING FOR THE WAVES

Together just once, wise in an instant,
they emerge from sand and shell fragments
riveted by the lowlight of stars,
by the cold brilliance, all the blues beyond instinct.
Thousands of tiny minds magnetically urged on
in a kind of grounded flight burning
with a fever, a drive to dazzle—as if there is time.
Each like a winged kiwi with flippers thin as peelings.
One stops to wipe sand from its eye.
The sky warns, the sinking of its sickle-moon is key.
The click-clockwork of migration nudges, shoves seaward.
The mind's what-ifs are comforted by the constant rustle
of nearby siblings, the trust, the rubbery scents,
newborn energy clambering, one over another.
Claws like just-cut fingernails give footholds
on skinny probabilities married to darkness.
Music of hurry dissolves against scale and skin
yoked to this frenzy fifty million years ago,
to the depths that cannot be fathomed.
Thousands will flail under the beaks
of ravens and gulls only slightly deterred
by gunfire from forest guards.
Thousands more will enter the hungry currents,
swallowing them whole. Will tumble in the roar,
hope tossed across a foamy elliptical.
Some will fly unencumbered,
bodies craving the low notes,
the rafts of seaweed and safety floating far
beyond imagination.

TURBIDITY

Our journey there is a hundred-and-seventy miles,
        a bullet train slicing through mustard fields,
ringing bicycles, road crossings crammed with cows,
        and guava stands. We wade into the Ganges,
touch the surface that carried my mother's ashes down
        fifteen years ago, leaving us stranded with her pearls,
silvers threaded through silks, great jars of lemons full of salts
        and sun, pickled to amber medicine. Instead
of staying with the silences, we fill time with logistics,
        apple-sized spiders, the hotel staff's antics.
A retired fashion designer emerges silked and cologned.
        Holding bougainvillea blooms to shade her lovely face,
she leans in, listens to my father. Crimson sunbirds hover
        as she laughs a cascade. Bank to bank, the Ganges River
is a quarter-mile wide, clarity clouded with glacial-blue flour,
        a roiling barely held beneath the surface. The guide
prepares novices like me with safety moves for the kayak.
        The river quickens to white. Walls of water shoot up
and collapse in a churning mass. The roaring splits direction
        into a million points of light. The kayak goes vertical.
Now it's far away, the guide shouting, reaching out to me
        with an oar. A bottomless stretch unravels memory,
and the world is finally calm. *There is water at the beginning of every idea,*
        my mother said. Before leaving the place, my father
suggests I help him write a sketch of her life as a sculptor.
        It's the first mention of her he's allowed himself.
I'm emptying wet sand out of my shoes. He's walking up the hill,
        cicadas ringing like phones he will not answer.

For I. P. Khosla

THE GIANT BUDDHAS OF BAMIYAN, AFGHANISTAN

Are long bombed. But even in their presence I knew
not to turn from the shouts taking aim, the gun
held high. Behind the boy-soldier, sculptures
the stuff of mountains held still, eyes closed.
He was bounding down, garbled babblings shooting
through wind. I am still racing away from the whip

of his voice. I did not run but tried to explain.
It was too late. His eyes were already narrowed.
Shards of war had already pierced his parents.
They might have taught him how to live,
to search for apples under the thump and whistle
of snow, to dare to be gentle.
Too late for him and other boy-orphans
kidnapped by a battalion of strangers,
marched to the front lines. Growing
with little to hold, more to hurl.
Setting land mines by night and taking turns
sleeping upright, leaning against cave walls
surrounded by smoke and a cloud of discipline.

It is years after that gun. Women who walked
without black veils were showered with the acid
from car batteries. They have washed, cooled,
and covered themselves. The Buddhas, five centuries
of prayer, are dust. They blessed us that day, two
bound for opposite sides of a war. One lowering
his gun, watching the other slide away in a car.

NIGHT OF THE LEATHERBACK

When she emerged from the tumbling foam we were jubilant
unaware that her presence was a star, spilling minimal brilliance,
lightyears away and burnt out. We had walked seven miles,
no other turtles. Only her tonnage heaving a Jurassic message,

sighs pungent with sea, the blind work of digging. Back flippers
kicked, sand flew at our eyes. Now the hollow, good for eggs
and birthing slime. She spilled them, then patted the sand
over seventy-five eggs, moved away to begin again.

A false nest, a final gesture of motherhood. Our good numbers
kept jackals and poachers from closing in. If words were possible,
we might have whispered about a time of balance between danger
and plenty. The world of watchful eyes and teeth

has never welcomed turtles whose gasps betray them,
but sheer numbers once overwhelmed the predators.
Now the darkness, sun's warmth daggering down
through historic cores of ice, us onlookers clinging to the edges
of a moment. Her crawl like bulldozer tracks. Something huge

finally driven to sea. And a shimmering spinal cord of water
running deeper than the reach of witness. As always,
the mangroves greeted light with faces wrapped in leafy scarves,
feet in sheets of tide. We touched the surface and felt only silk.

Little Andaman Island, 2011

DISENTANGLING A GRAY WHALE

Water minus air becomes wound.
Her blowhole, bursts of breathing,
trapped in an endless curtain of netting
and weights designed to confine tuna.
She tries to surface. The body greater
than two double-decker buses in length
and girth. We close in, hesitant,

wondering if freeing her is worth the risk
of a nervous tail slap into oblivion. After all,
she may be too far behind to sing her way
back to the rest of her pod.
Song bouncing from underwater canyon

to canyon mapped by sound and echo.
She may not endow us with any answers
to the sea of unknowns. She may be one
of the strays deafened into idiocy

by the Navy's sonic booms
clocking the globe with the constancy
of gunfire. She may simply be
an upshot, a bulbous, barnacled emblem

of our earth-ship's sinking—
the grimace of her mouth
not unlike her blue gods miles below
holding their own while bubbles of breath
are spiraling up like prayers for salvation.

ALL THE FIRES OF WIND AND LIGHT

This morning, a monarch butterfly—
leaf-blown clear across the beloved lands
where forests tire and ready

themselves to uncloak en masse.
I search for more, through milkweeds,
willows, filigrees of grassy sun.

But no—it's just this one.
Leap of faith taken, arrival treasured.
Black and blood-orange wings

slightly tattered along the edges
report her journey here as no small matter.
All the fires of wind and light and darkness

shot through with stars
were guide and adversary to her will.
Flying, she felt the days grow brittle thin

and fall to the ground behind her.
Well, here she is, all grace and restraint
alighting where the sugars of fall

have tightened into berries. A reminder
that despite the ache of leading
a loved one's ashes to a river,

despite the sand and wet drops
clinging to fingers like regret,
the spirit flows on with elegance.

NOTES

"Amazing Grace": The nine men and women who lost their lives in the 2015 Charleston church massacre were Cynthia Marie Graham Hurd, Susie Jackson, Ethel Lee Lance, Depayne Middleton-Doctor, Clementa C. Pinckney, Tywanza Sanders, Daniel Simmons, Sharonda Coleman-Singleton, and Myra Thompson.

"Quilting, a Refugee Remembers Her Home Before the Dam Was Built": India's Narmada Dam is one of many large-scale development projects. Construction began in 1987, and the dam eventually displaced hundreds of thousands of people from their native homelands. Several of the women who were among the families forced to move began working as seamstresses in Kumbaya, a nonprofit group based in the remote village of Baagli, in the state of Madhya Pradesh.

ACKNOWLEDGMENTS

Grateful acknowledgment is made to the editors of the following publications, which featured versions of these poems:

California Quarterly: "All the Fires of Wind and Light"; *Canary*: "Girls Wandering Through a Mustard Field," "Sea Turtles Arrive," "Crash of Rhinos," "Cloaks of Charcoal"; *Chicago Quarterly Review*: "Thumbprint," "Clingstone"; *Munyori Journal*: "Sea Turtles Arrive," "In Kabul," "Yuba River"; *Poem*: "Smoke-Detecting Beetles"; *Prairie Schooner*: "Synchronicity"; *Reflections, Yale Divinity School*: "Amazing Grace"; *Rhino*: "New Year Between Countries"; *The Literary Review*: "Reuse and Renewal," "Golden Eagle," "Band-Tailed Pigeons After the Storm"; *The Press Democrat*: "Rejuvenation"; *Weber: The Contemporary West*: "Injury," "In Kabul"; *World Literature*

Today: "Disentangling a Gray Whale," "After Donating One of Her Kidneys," "Dispersal"

"Golden Eagle" won the Free Verse Poetry Prize from *Byline Magazine*.

"Dispersal" and "After Donating One of Her Kidneys," featured in *World Literature Today*, were nominated for Pushcart Prizes.

"Synchronicity," "Half a Sentence," and "A Poet's Keystone" were published in *The Harper Collins Book of English Poetry* (2012).

"Deforestation" was published in *Indivisible: An Anthology of South Asian American Poetry* (University of Arkansas Press, 2010).

"Translation" and "Blackbirds in a Bare Tree at Dusk" were published in *Fog and Woodsmoke* (Lost Hills Press, 2011).

"Translation" and "*Giganteum*, the Redwood" were featured in *Digging Our Poetic Roots: Poems from Sonoma County,* Katherine Hastings, ed. (WordTemple Press, 2015).

"Pilgrimage to Cow's Mouth Mountain" was published in *Collective Brightness* (Sibling Rivalry Press, 2011).

"Subsidence" was published in The Nevada County Poetry Series Year 2004 Anthology.

Many thanks to Sanskriti Kala Kendra, Hedgebrook, and the Headlands Center for the Arts for giving spaces where *All the Fires of Wind and Light* was completed.

ABOUT THE AUTHOR

Maya Khosla is the poet laureate of Sonoma County (2018–20). Her work in the natural world has led her into the wild, to the page, and to the screen. Her other books of poetry are *Keel Bone* (Bear Star Press) and *Heart of the Tearing* (Red Dust Press), and she is the author of a guidebook, *Web of Water: Life in Redwood Creek*. Her film *Searching for the Gold Spot*, which received a star pick from *Library Journal*, is devoted to wild places that grow to support high biodiversity after natural wildfire.

Sixteen Rivers Press is a shared-work, nonprofit poetry collective
dedicated to providing an alternative publishing avenue
for Northern California poets. Founded in 1999
by seven writers, the press is named
for the sixteen rivers that flow into San Francisco Bay.

SAN JOAQUIN • FRESNO • CHOWCHILLA • MERCED • TUOLUMNE
STANISLAUS • CALAVERAS • BEAR • MOKELUMNE • COSUMNES
AMERICAN • YUBA • FEATHER • SACRAMENTO • NAPA • PETALUMA